STRANGE SCIENCE

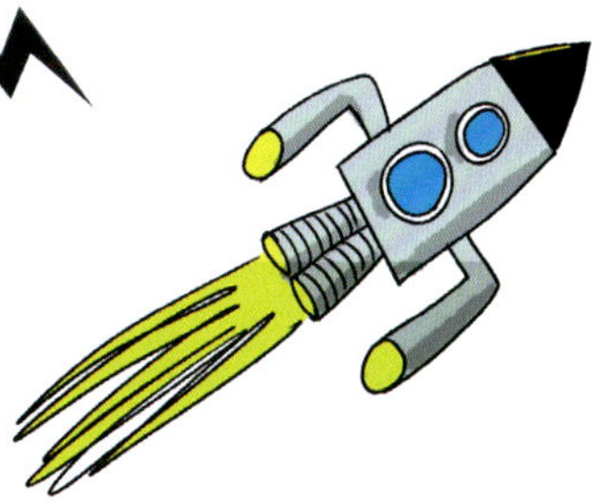

HOW DO STARS TURN INTO SPAGHETTI?

BY ANNA CLAYBOURNE
AND TIM WESSON

Gareth Stevens
PUBLISHING

Please visit our website, www.garethstevens.com. For a free color catalog of all our high-quality books, call toll free 1-800-542-2595 or fax 1-877-542-2596.

Cataloging-in-Publication Data
Names: Claybourne, Anna. | Wesson, Tim.
Title: How do stars turn into spaghetti? / by Anna Claybourne and Tim Wesson.
Description: Buffalo, NY : Gareth Stevens Publishing, 2027. | Series: Strange science | Includes glossary and index.
Identifiers: ISBN 9781482478310 (pbk.) | ISBN 9781482478327 (library bound) | ISBN 9781482478334 (ebook)
Subjects: LCSH: Astronomy--Miscellanea--Juvenile literature. | Solar system--Miscellanea--Juvenile literature. | Outer space--Miscellanea--Juvenile literature. | Outer space--Exploration--Juvenile literature.
Classification: LCC QB46.C53 2027 | DDC 520.2--dc23

Published in 2027 by
Gareth Stevens Publishing
2544 Clinton St.
Buffalo, NY 14224

First published in Great Britain in 2025 by wayland

Commissioning editor: Melanie Palmer
Designer: Lisa Peacock

Printed in China
CPSIA compliance information: Batch #QS27GS: For further information contact Gareth Stevens at 1-800-542-2595.

Find us on

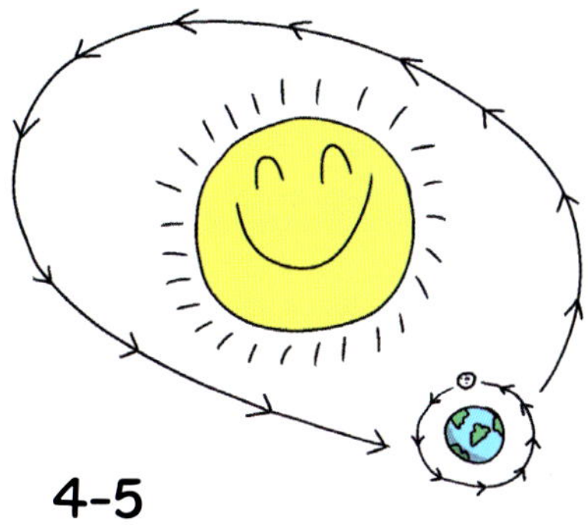

CONTENTS

THE SILLY SCIENCE OF SPACE

Hi there! It's me, Professor Splat. I'm here to show you around a very strange place ... called space!
Meow!
Let's find out what space really means!

WHAT IS SPACE?

SPACE BASICALLY MEANS THE WHOLE UNIVERSE BEYOND OUR PLANET, EARTH. AND THE UNIVERSE IS EVERYTHING THAT EXISTS!

IT'S CALLED "SPACE" BECAUSE IT'S VERY BIG, AND THERE'S LOTS OF ... WELL ... SPACE!

DOTTED AROUND IN ALL THAT SPACE ARE LOTS OF INTERESTING BITS AND PIECES.

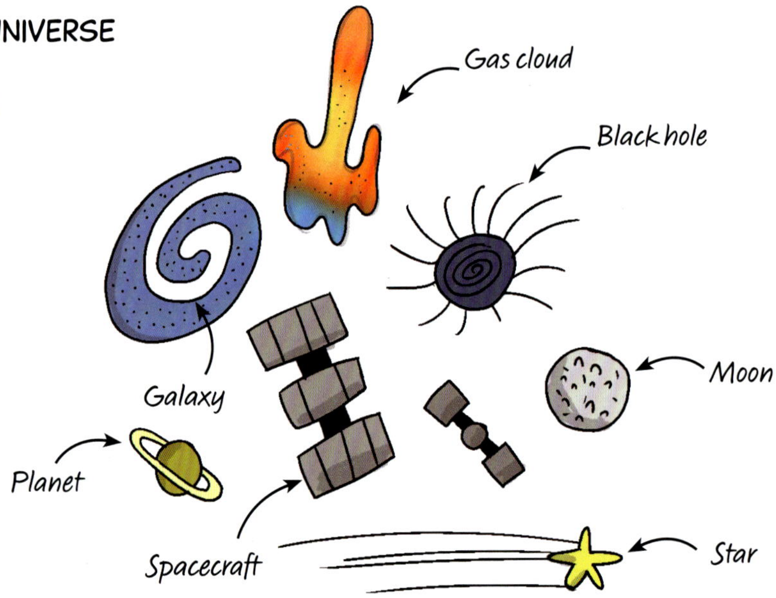
Gas cloud
Black hole
Galaxy
Moon
Planet
Spacecraft
Star

A LOT OF SILLY, FUNNY, AND SERIOUSLY STRANGE THINGS HAPPEN IN SPACE. FOR EXAMPLE, DID YOU KNOW THAT ...

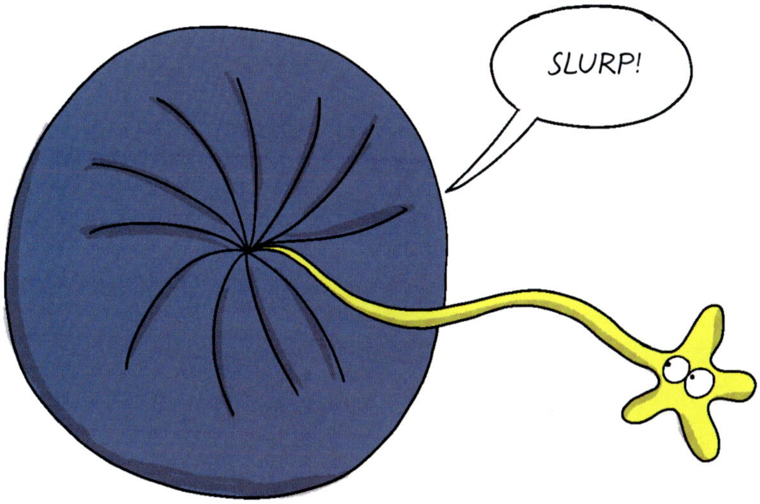
SLURP!

• A black hole can turn stars into spaghetti ...

• playing a saxophone in space can blow you away ...

PARP!

• and you're zooming through space at millions of miles per hour – right now!

Am I?
Meow!

SO MANY QUESTIONS!

WHICH PLANET HAS A POPULATION OF ROBOTS?

HOW DO SPACE TOILETS STOP POOP FROM ESCAPING?

WHY DID SPACE START WITH A BANG?

To find out, float this way!

IT STARTED WITH A BANGGG!

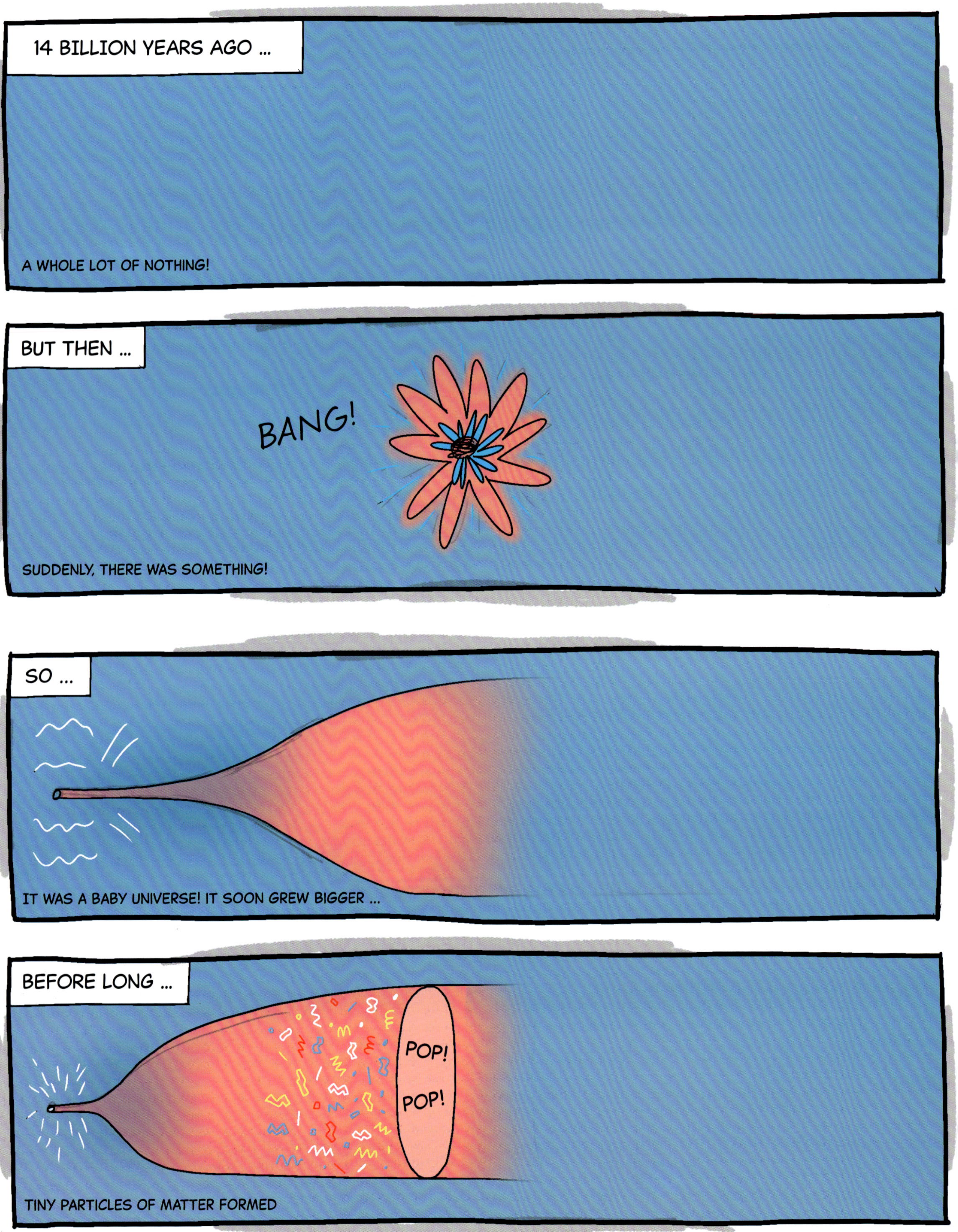
14 BILLION YEARS AGO ...
A WHOLE LOT OF NOTHING!
BUT THEN ...
BANG!
SUDDENLY, THERE WAS SOMETHING!
SO ...
IT WAS A BABY UNIVERSE! IT SOON GREW BIGGER ...
BEFORE LONG ...
POP!
POP!
TINY PARTICLES OF MATTER FORMED

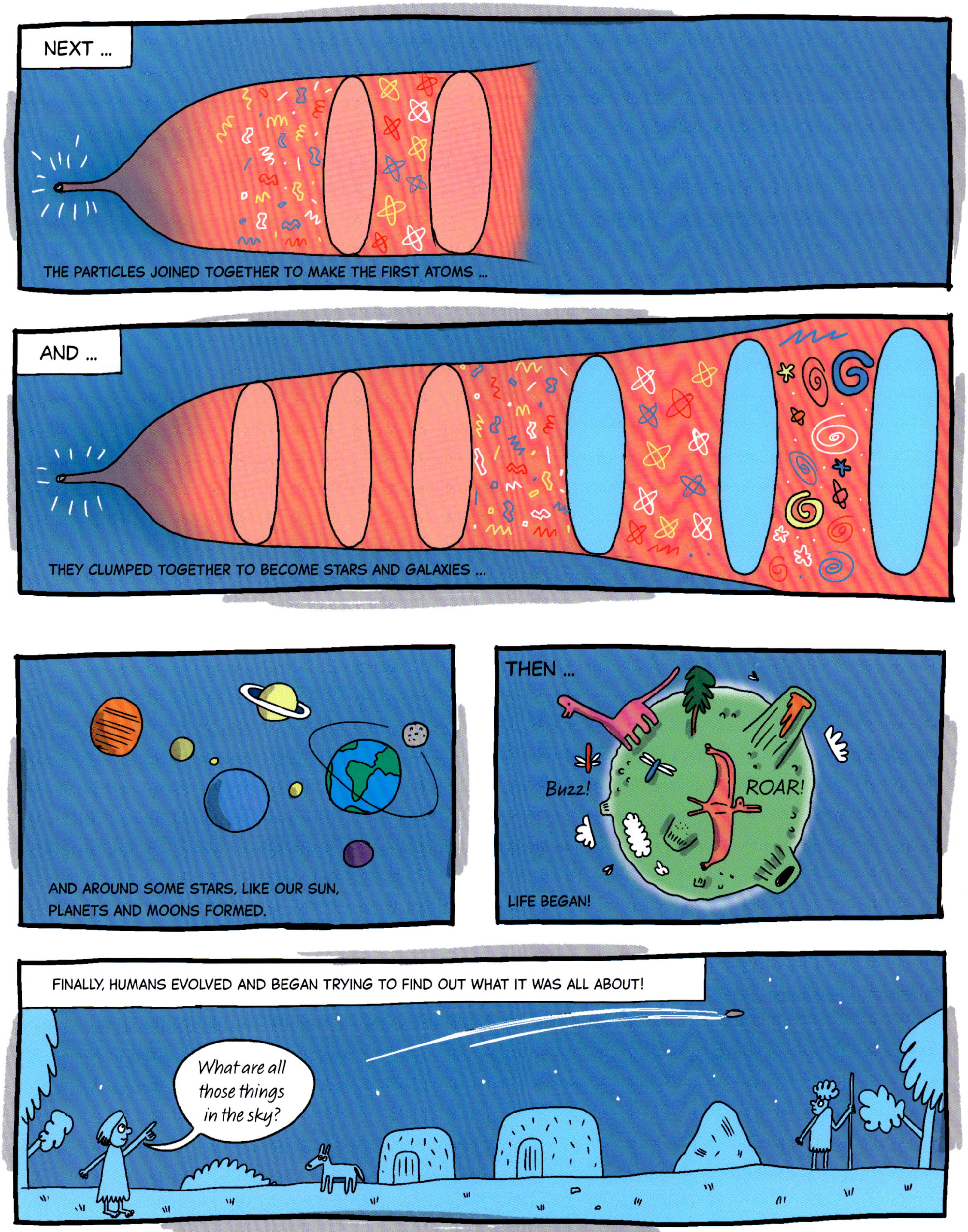
NEXT ...
THE PARTICLES JOINED TOGETHER TO MAKE THE FIRST ATOMS ...
AND ...
THEY CLUMPED TOGETHER TO BECOME STARS AND GALAXIES ...
AND AROUND SOME STARS, LIKE OUR SUN, PLANETS AND MOONS FORMED.
THEN ...
Buzz!
ROAR!
LIFE BEGAN!
FINALLY, HUMANS EVOLVED AND BEGAN TRYING TO FIND OUT WHAT IT WAS ALL ABOUT!
What are all those things in the sky?

WHAT IS IT ALL ABOUT?

DID IT START WITH A BANG?

WHERE DID THE UNIVERSE COME FROM, AND HOW DID IT BEGIN? WE CAN'T BE SURE, BECAUSE NO ONE WAS THERE! HUMANS DIDN'T EXIST UNTIL MUCH, MUCH LATER.

That's a good question. Space is VERY mysterious ...
Let me take a look!

BUT SPACE SCIENTISTS HAVE SPOTTED THAT THE STARS AND GALAXIES SEEM TO BE MOVING APART, AND THE UNIVERSE IS GETTING BIGGER – KIND OF LIKE A BALLOON BEING BLOWN UP.

SCIENTISTS THINK THAT MEANS IT MUST HAVE STARTED OFF FROM A SINGLE, TINY POINT, ABOUT 13.8 BILLION YEARS AGO. ALL THE MATTER, OR STUFF, IN THE UNIVERSE JUST EXPLODED OUT OF NOTHING – WHICH WE NOW CALL THE "BIG BANG."

But why?
Erm ... Nobody knows.
And what was there before?
Erm ... Nothing.
How can something come out of nothing?
Erm ... I don't know.

CONFUSED?

IT IS VERY CONFUSING – AND EVEN SPACE SCIENTISTS DON'T KNOW IF IT'S DEFINITELY TRUE. IT'S A THEORY – THE BEST GUESS WE HAVE, BASED ON THE EVIDENCE.

SOME SCIENTISTS HAVE DIFFERENT THEORIES, SUCH AS...

There was no Big Bang – the universe just keeps growing and shrinking!
THE BIG BOUNCE
Ouch!
No ... ours is just one of countless universes, all popping in and out of existence!
THE MULTIVERSE
Nonsense! There's just one other universe – a mirror-image version joined onto ours!
THE MIRRORVERSE
Now I'm even more confused.
This isn't helping!

BUT THESE ARE ALL JUST THEORIES TOO. NO ONE KNOWS FOR SURE!

ANCIENT ASTRONOMY

THOUSANDS OF YEARS AGO ...
The sky looks pretty!
Yes, the moon is big!
Stars are shining!

ANCIENT PEOPLE OFTEN WATCHED THE NIGHT SKY ...

How do they stay up? Everything else falls down – like tree leaves and rain!

... BUT THEY DIDN'T REALLY KNOW WHAT IT WAS OR HOW IT WORKED!

Because they're stuck on, silly!
Stuck onto what?

Stuck onto the sky! The sky is a big roof, like an upside down bowl, made of metal.

THEY DID TRY TO FIGURE OUT HOW IT WORKED ...

No, I think it's made of stone! And the stars aren't stuck to it. They're just little holes that the light shines through.
No, no, that's all wrong! The stars are little lanterns hanging on the sky. There are little holes, but they're for letting the rain through!
What about the moon and sun then? Why do they move around?
They roll, obviously!
EVENTUALLY ...
None of this makes much sense!

DIFFERENT ANCIENT PEOPLES ALL HAD THEIR OWN IDEAS – BUT THEY WERE MOSTLY WRONG!

THE STORY OF SPACE SCIENCE

As we now know, the sky is NOT a solid dome with little holes in it! If it was, space rockets wouldn't get very far, would they?

DONK!

GUESSING GAME

IT WAS HARD FOR EARLY PEOPLE TO UNDERSTAND SPACE. THERE WERE NO TELESCOPES, AND NO SPACE TRAVEL. MANY PEOPLE THOUGHT EARTH WAS FLAT, AS NO ONE HAD SAILED ALL THE WAY AROUND IT IN ANCIENT TIMES.

LITTLE DID THEY KNOW THEY WERE SITTING ON A GIANT BALL OF ROCK, LOOKING OUT INTO THE VASTNESS OF SPACE ... AT STARS THAT WERE MILLIONS OR BILLIONS OF MILES AWAY!

So they could only guess what was really going on in the sky!

SPACE DISCOVERIES

BUT THE MORE WE WATCHED THE SKIES, THE MORE WE FIGURED OUT ...

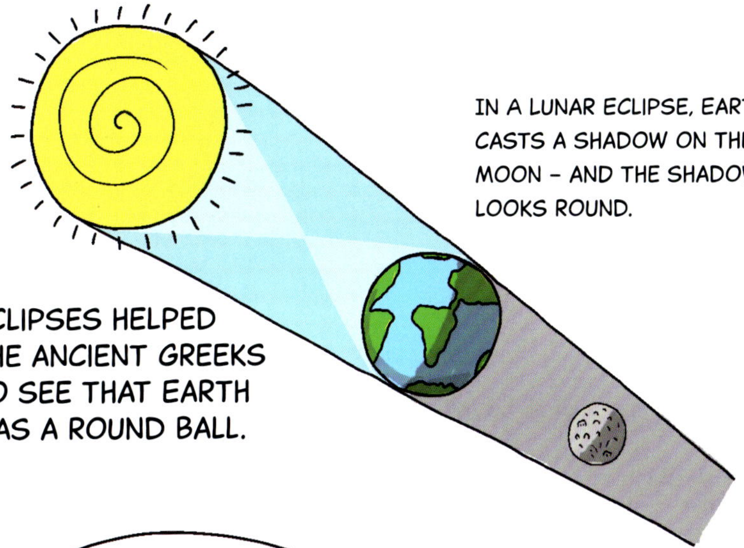

IN A LUNAR ECLIPSE, EARTH CASTS A SHADOW ON THE MOON – AND THE SHADOW LOOKS ROUND.

ECLIPSES HELPED THE ANCIENT GREEKS TO SEE THAT EARTH WAS A ROUND BALL.

PEOPLE REALIZED THAT SOME STARS MOVED IN A DIFFERENT WAY FROM THE REST. THEY WERE PLANETS!

COPERNICUS

The planets move around in a very odd pattern. It only makes sense if they're moving around the sun, not Earth.

IN THE 1500S, COPERNICUS REALIZED EARTH WASN'T IN THE MIDDLE OF EVERYTHING. IN FACT, ALL THE PLANETS MOVED AROUND THE SUN!

Oooh look at that! Jupiter has lots of moons!

GALILEO

AND WHEN TELESCOPES WERE INVENTED, WE FOUND OUT EVEN MORE ABOUT THE MOON, THE PLANETS, AND FARAWAY STARS.

GALILEO WAS THE FIRST TO REALIZE THAT EARTH WASN'T THE ONLY PLANET WITH A MOON.

TRAVELING WITHOUT MOVING?

You're moving fast!
I'm not moving at all. I'm just having a nice nap!
DID YOU KNOW...
We're all actually moving all the time, as Earth spins, orbits the sun, and flies through space!
SPIN! Wheee!
EARTH SPINS ONCE EVERY 24 HOURS. AT THE EQUATOR, YOU'LL TRAVEL 25,000 MILES (40,000 KM) IN THAT TIME, OR 1,000 MILES PER HOUR (1,670 KM/H). ON AVERAGE, WE ZOOM AROUND AT 620 MILES PER HOUR (1,000 KM/H).
BUT THERE'S MORE ...
WHOOSH! Woah!
MEANWHILE, EARTH IS ORBITING AROUND THE SUN AT 66,500 MILES PER HOUR (107,000 KM/H)!

THE SOLAR SYSTEM
AND MORE ...
WHIRL! Yikes!
AND THE WHOLE SOLAR SYSTEM – THAT'S THE SUN AND ALL ITS PLANETS – IS MOVING TOO!
AND MORE!
ZOOOOOOM! Woof!
AND THE MILKY WAY GALAXY ITSELF IS MOVING THROUGH SPACE AT 1.2 MILLION MILES PER HOUR (1.9 MILLION KM/H)!
SO IN TOTAL ...
... you're flying through space over 435 miles (700 km) every second.
AND IT'S WIGGLY TOO!
I feel dizzy now!
SO WHY CAN'T YOU FEEL IT?
But I don't feel like I'm moving at all!
That's because Earth's atmosphere is moving with you.

SPINNING AROUND

MOVING UNIVERSE

IT'S NOT JUST EARTH THAT MOVES. EVERYTHING IN SPACE IS MOVING.

That's another amazing thing about space! It's not just some faraway place. We're zooming through it all the time!

PLANETS ORBIT AROUND STARS ...

MOONS ORBIT AROUND PLANETS ...

STARS WHIRL AROUND IN GIANT GALAXIES ...

Look out!

COMETS, ASTEROIDS, AND SPACE DUST ZOOM AROUND TOO.

IN ORBIT

IN SPACE, OBJECTS ORBIT AROUND OTHER OBJECTS BECAUSE OF GRAVITY. BUT HOW DOES THAT WORK!?

Here's how. Let me explain ...

It's simple!
All space objects have gravity.

THE MORE MASS, OR STUFF, AN OBJECT HAS IN IT, THE STRONGER ITS GRAVITY – LIKE THIS BIG PLANET.

Big planets like Jupiter can have lots of moons.

I can't escape – but I don't fall either!
I just keep going around and around ...

GRAVITY PULLS ON OTHER OBJECTS, LIKE THIS MOON AROUND JUPITER, BUT THE MOON IS ZOOMING ALONG AT HIGH SPEED, MAKING IT TRY TO PULL AWAY. THE TWO FORCES BALANCE, AND THE MOON ENDS UP MOVING AROUND THE PLANET.

IN A SPIN

MOST SPACE OBJECTS ARE SPINNING TOO. BUT WHY?

LONG AGO, AFTER THE BIG BANG, GRAVITY PULLED ATOMS TOGETHER TO FORM THINGS LIKE ROCKS.

THEN ROCKS CLUMPED TOGETHER TO MAKE BIGGER THINGS LIKE PLANETS AND MOONS.

I think we're going to crash!
Grab my hand!

OBJECTS USUALLY CRASH TOGETHER UNEVENLY OR AT AN ANGLE, MAKING THEM SPIN.

Aarrggh!
We're spinning!

THE BIGGEST STAR

HAVE YOU EVER MET A STAR?
I'm a big star, you know!
IT'S TRUE, THE SUN IS PRETTY BIG! IT'S 870,000 MILES (1.4 MILLION KM) ACROSS – OVER 100 TIMES WIDER THAN EARTH.
And I'm also very bright.
THE SUN GIVES OUT SO MUCH HEAT AND LIGHT, IT WARMS UP EARTH – EVEN THOUGH WE'RE 91 MILLION MILES (147 MILLION KM) AWAY!
There can't be any stars as big, bright, and beautiful as me!
AHEM! That's where you're wrong!
Hello, little Sun!

GULP! Who are you?
I'm Rigel, and I'm MUCH bigger than you!
I'm also a beautiful bright blue!
RIGEL IS OVER 62 MILLION MILES (100 MILLION KM) WIDE AND 120,000 TIMES BRIGHTER THAN THE SUN!
EXCUSE ME!
Wow. That's a REALLY big star.
I am Betelgeuse. I'm a SUPERGIANT!
I guess I'm not such a big star after all.
You're still my favorite star - you're perfect as you are!

SECRETS OF THE STARS

WHEN YOU LOOK AT THE NIGHT SKY, THE STARS ALL LOOK QUITE SIMILAR. SMALL, AND TWINKLY!

BUT TELESCOPES REVEAL HOW DIFFERENT THEY CAN BE!

THEY COME IN A HUGE RANGE OF SIZES, WITH DIFFERENT TEMPERATURES, BRIGHTNESSES, AGES, AND EVEN COLORS.

What a beautiful night! So many stars.
And with my telescope, we can get a really good look at them all!

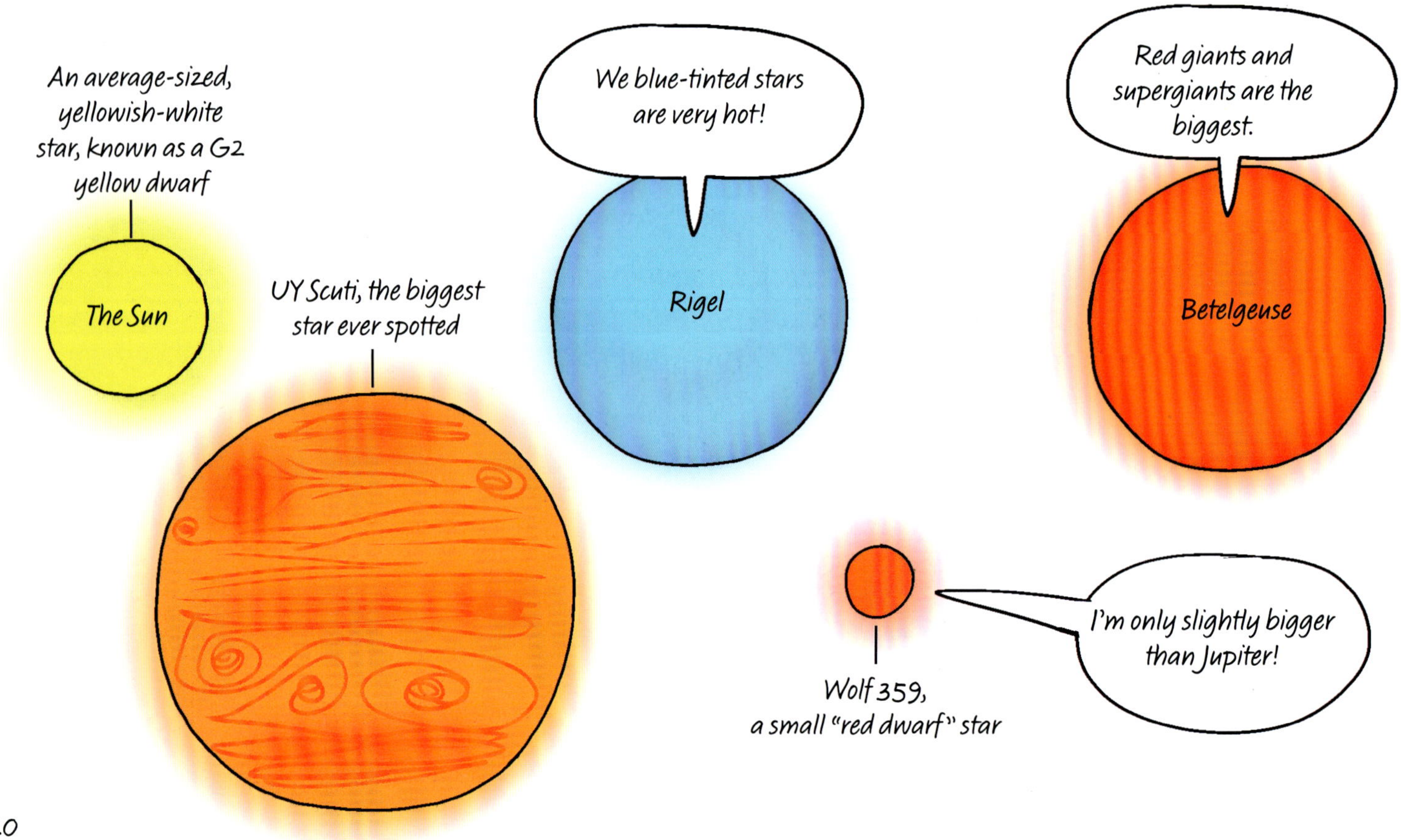
An average-sized, yellowish-white star, known as a G2 yellow dwarf
The Sun
UY Scuti, the biggest star ever spotted
We blue-tinted stars are very hot!
Rigel
Red giants and supergiants are the biggest.
Betelgeuse
I'm only slightly bigger than Jupiter!
Wolf 359, a small "red dwarf" star

LIFE OF A STAR

Stars aren't really alive – but they do have a lifetime! They form as a ball of hot, exploding gases, change as they get older, then burn out!
Nooooo! We're doomed!
Don't worry … it takes billions of years!

BIGGER STARS LIKE BETELGEUSE BECOME RED SUPERGIANTS, THEN BLOW UP IN A HUGE EXPLOSION CALLED A SUPERNOVA. THEN THEY MAY TURN INTO A BLACK HOLE!

A STAR LIKE THE SUN WILL GROW INTO A RED GIANT, THEN COLLAPSE, AND BECOME A WHITE DWARF.

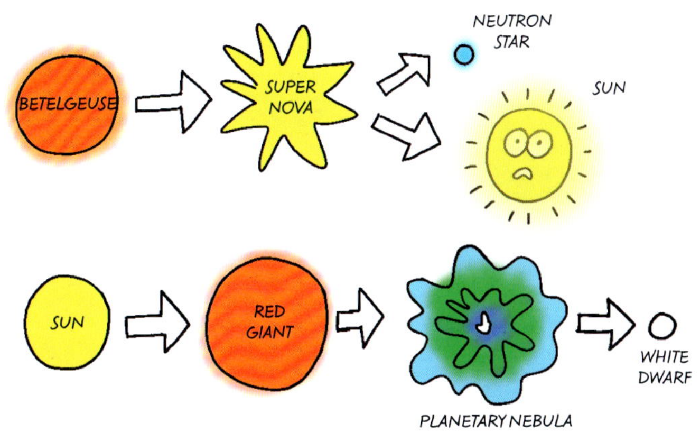
BETELGEUSE
SUPER NOVA
NEUTRON STAR
SUN
SUN
RED GIANT
PLANETARY NEBULA
WHITE DWARF

A black hole? What's that?
You're about to find out …
Prepare for some weirdness!

STAR SPAGHETTI

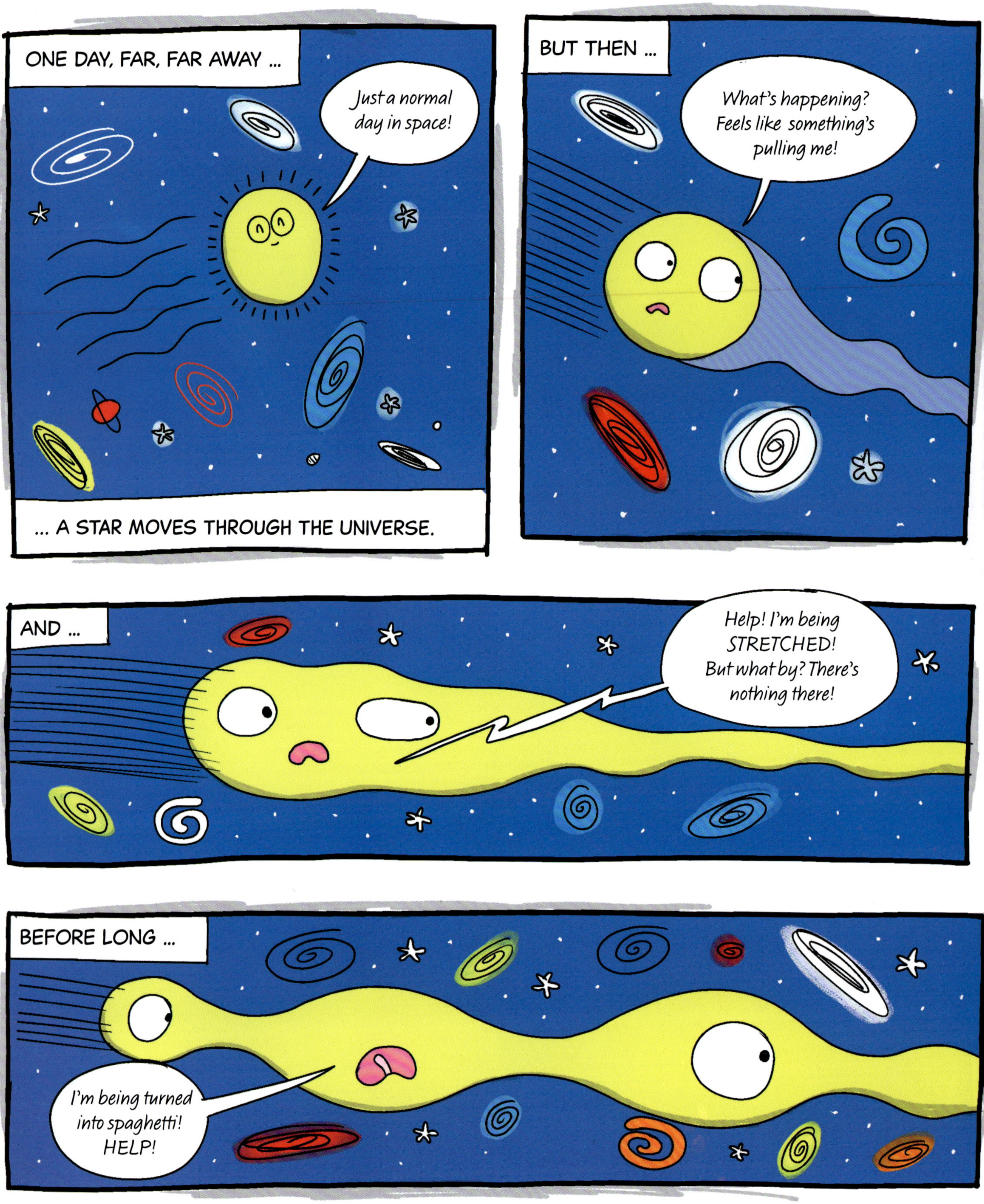
ONE DAY, FAR, FAR AWAY ...
Just a normal day in space!
... A STAR MOVES THROUGH THE UNIVERSE.
BUT THEN ...
What's happening? Feels like something's pulling me!
AND ...
Help! I'm being STRETCHED! But what by? There's nothing there!
BEFORE LONG ...
I'm being turned into spaghetti! HELP!

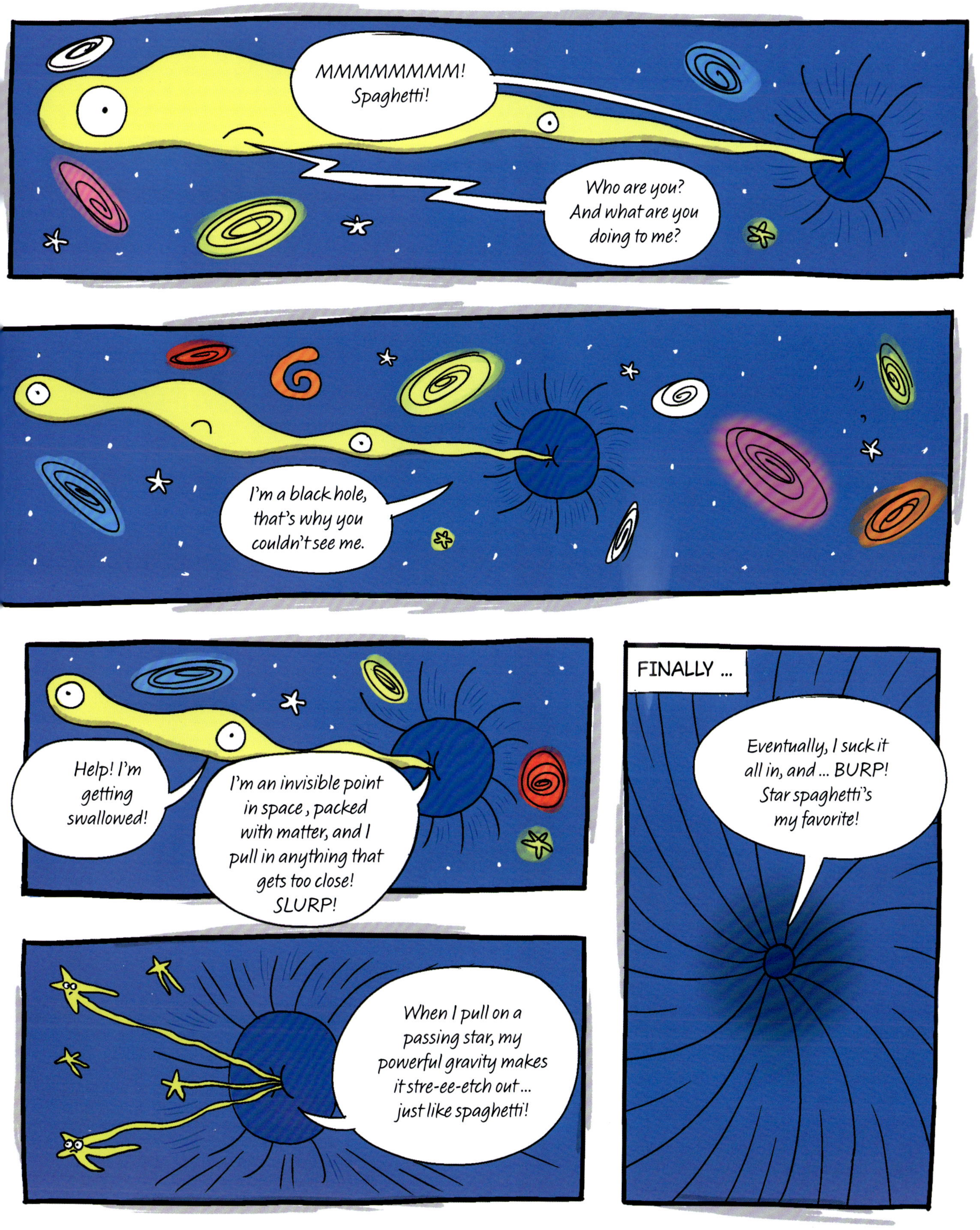
MMMMMMMMM! Spaghetti!
Who are you? And what are you doing to me?
I'm a black hole, that's why you couldn't see me.
Help! I'm getting swallowed!
I'm an invisible point in space, packed with matter, and I pull in anything that gets too close! SLURP!
When I pull on a passing star, my powerful gravity makes it stre-ee-etch out... just like spaghetti!
FINALLY ...
Eventually, I suck it all in, and ... BURP! Star spaghetti's my favorite!

IMPOSSIBLE HOLES IN SPACE

You do NOT want to get sucked in by a black hole!
HELP!
Feed me!

WHAT ARE BLACK HOLES?

BLACK HOLES ARE VERY STRANGE, HARD-TO-UNDERSTAND SPACE OBJECTS. HERE'S WHAT HAPPENS ...

CORE

AS A GIANT STAR GETS OLD, IRON COLLECTS IN THE MIDDLE OR CORE.

EVENTUALLY, THIS MAKES THE STAR IMPLODE ...

… LEADING TO A GIANT EXPLOSION, CALLED A SUPERNOVA.

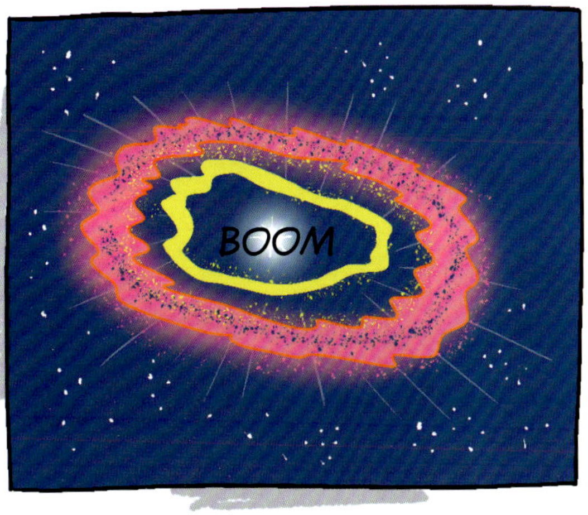
BOOM

Then the star collapses into a black hole

IN A BLACK HOLE, ALL THE MATTER, OR STUFF, FROM THE STAR'S CORE IS SO TIGHTLY SQUISHED TOGETHER, IT TAKES UP NO SPACE AT ALL!!

IT'S JUST A DOT – A SINGLE POINT IN SPACE.

BUT IT HAS STRONG GRAVITY THAT PULLS THINGS INTO IT.

TURNING INTO SPAGHETTI

WHEN A STAR, OR ANYTHING ELSE, GETS CLOSE TO A BLACK HOLE, THE GRAVITY MAKES IT STRETCH OUT INTO A LONG STRING AS IT GETS SUCKED IN.

IT'S CALLED SPAGHETTIFICATION!

That doesn't make sense! How can all that matter be inside an invisible dot?
We don't know! But it's the best guess we have for how black holes work.

POOP ON THE LOOSE!

MAY 18, 1969 ...
5 ... 4 ... 3 ... 2 ... 1 ... we have lift-off!
THE APOLLO 10 MISSION SET OFF TO FLY AROUND THE MOON, TO PREPARE FOR THE FIRST MOON LANDING LATER THAT YEAR.
A FEW DAYS LATER ...
Mission successful! Time to head home!
THE APOLLO 10 MISISION GETS READY TO RETURN BACK TO EARTH.
BUT THEN ...
What is THAT?
There!
It looks like a POOP!

SO ...
Who did it!?
It wasn't me!
Well, it definitely wasn't ME!
Better catch it and trash it! Can't have poops floating around!
FINALLY ...
Well, it's not surprising really.
POOP BAG
Our toilets are basically plastic bags! A bit must have fallen out!
We need to invent some better space toilets ... in time for our next mission!

SPACE TOILETS

In the 1960s, space scientists built spacecraft that could go to the moon and come back safely ...
But sadly they didn't make the space toilets so high-tech!
POO BAGS

WHAT'S THE PROBLEM?

THE PROBLEM IS THAT WHEN YOU'RE IN SPACE, YOU'RE IN MICROGRAVITY, AND FLOAT AROUND ALL OVER THE PLACE. AND SO DOES EVERYTHING ELSE – LIKE FOOD, TOOLS, PENCILS ... AND POOP!

TODAY'S SUPER-ADVANCED SPACE TOILETS, USED ON THE INTERNATIONAL SPACE STATION, HAVE SUCTION POWER.

You can't use a toilet like the ones on Earth. The water and waste would just float out of it!

As soon as you sit down, the suction starts. Pee and poo get sucked away into sealed containers so they can't get out.

POOPING STARS

WHAT HAPPENS TO ASTRONAUTS' PEE AND POO?

THE PEE GETS COLLECTED AND CLEANED, THEN RECYCLED INTO FRESH DRINKING WATER!

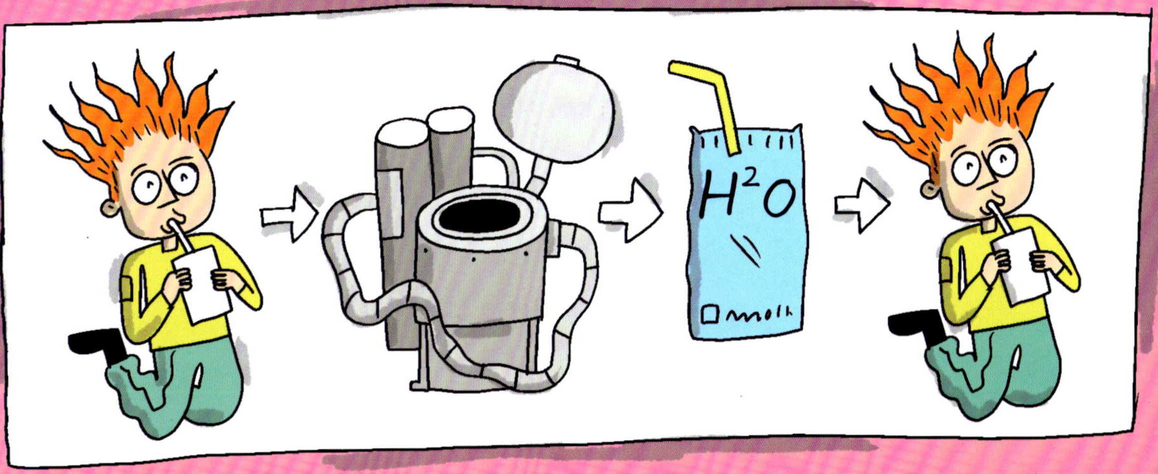

MEANWHILE, THE POOP IS STORED IN BAGS THAT ARE LOADED ON TO A SPECIAL SPACE MODULE.

WHEN IT'S FULL OF POOP AND OTHER TRASH, IT'S FIRED TOWARD EARTH. IT BURNS UP IN THE ATMOSPHERE, BECOMING A METEOR, OR SHOOTING STAR.

SAXOPHONES IN SPACE

ON BOARD THE INTERNATIONAL SPACE STATION ...
That's all my experiments done. Time for a break!
DECK
Why don't we play some music to relax ...
DECK
SO ...
That sounds great! I'll play my guitar.
THEN ...
Ooh! Can I join in? I brought my saxophone!

BUT ...
PARRP!!!
CRASH!
Are you OK?
You need something to hold you still! The air coming out of the sax is pushing you backwards!
SO ...
I'll stick my feet in here! Perfect.
PARRP!!!
Hey, we sound great!

FLOATING FREE

Whooo ... floating around in space is so much fun! But it CAN cause a few problems ...

MICROGRAVITY

WHEN ASTRONAUTS ARE ON A SPACE STATION ORBITING EARTH, THEY DON'T FEEL GRAVITY. THEY'RE IN WHAT'S KNOWN AS "MICROGRAVITY."

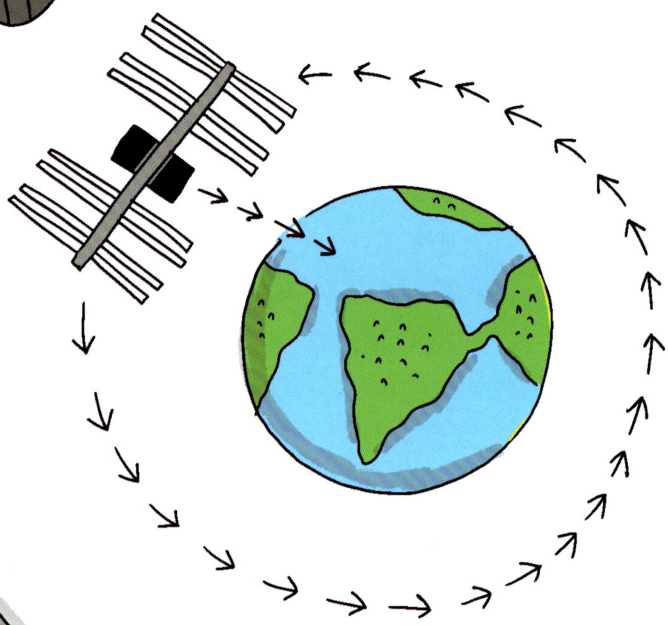

Wheeee! There's no "down" on a space station.

EARTH'S GRAVITY IS WEAKER, BUT STILL PULLS ON THEM. HOWEVER, AS THE ASTRONAUTS AND THE SPACE STATION ARE BOTH IN ORBIT TOGETHER, THEY DON'T FEEL IT. THEY JUST FLOAT AROUND INSIDE THE CABIN.

BUT ...

IT'S NOT ALL FUN AND GAMES ...

Your food can float away!

You have to fasten yourself into your bed, or you'd drift around in your sleep and bump into things!

It's even difficult to burp, as gas doesn't rise up in your throat like it does on Earth.

And if you blow air out, it makes you move backward!

ACTIVATE THRUSTERS

Activate thrusters to turn upside-down!

SPACECRAFT OFTEN USE THIS METHOD TO MOVE AROUND AND CHANGE THEIR POSITION IN SPACE.

THRUSTERS SHOOT OUT JETS OF GAS.

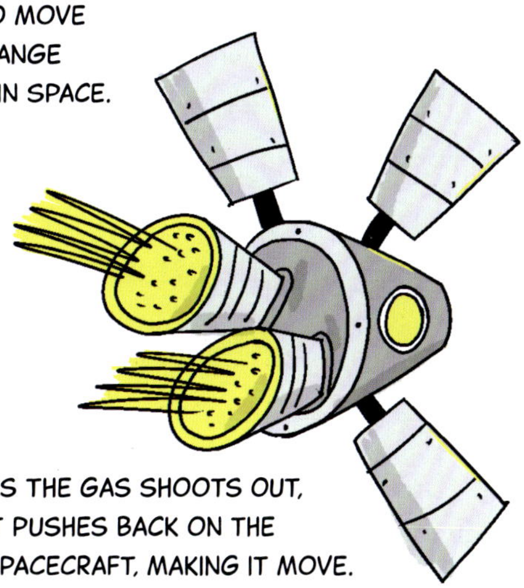

AS THE GAS SHOOTS OUT, IT PUSHES BACK ON THE SPACECRAFT, MAKING IT MOVE.

ROBOT WORLD

FEBRUARY 18, 2021, ON THE PLANET MARS ...
Are we nearly there yet?
THE ROBOT ROVER PERSEVERANCE IS ABOUT TO LAND ON MARS.
A FEW MINUTES LATER ...
I'm landing! Wow, Mars looks amazing! Time to start exploring and studying rocks!
This is fun! But a bit lonely ...
Oh, you're not alone!
I'm Curiosity! I've been here for years! I'm similar to you – but you're a bit more high-tech.

We're twins! I'm Spirit ...
... and I'm Opportunity! We arrived in 2004.
I'm Sojourner. I may look small and simple, but I was the first robot rover on Mars, back in 1997!
Incoming!
And there are even more rovers on the way!
Why don't humans just come here?
Humans wouldn't survive the cold nights or lack of air. Robots rule on Mars!

NO HUMANS, NO PROBLEM!

Mars is one of the closest planets to Earth – but it's still a LONG way away. That's why, so far, only robots have been able to go.
In fact, Mars is the only planet that's populated entirely by robots!

ROBOT EXPLORERS

ROBOT ROVERS LIKE PERSEVERANCE HAVE LOTS OF EQUIPMENT FOR FINDING THEIR WAY, TAKING PICTURES, AND STUDYING MARS'S ROCKS AND SOIL.

FOR EXAMPLE, PERSEVERANCE HAS:

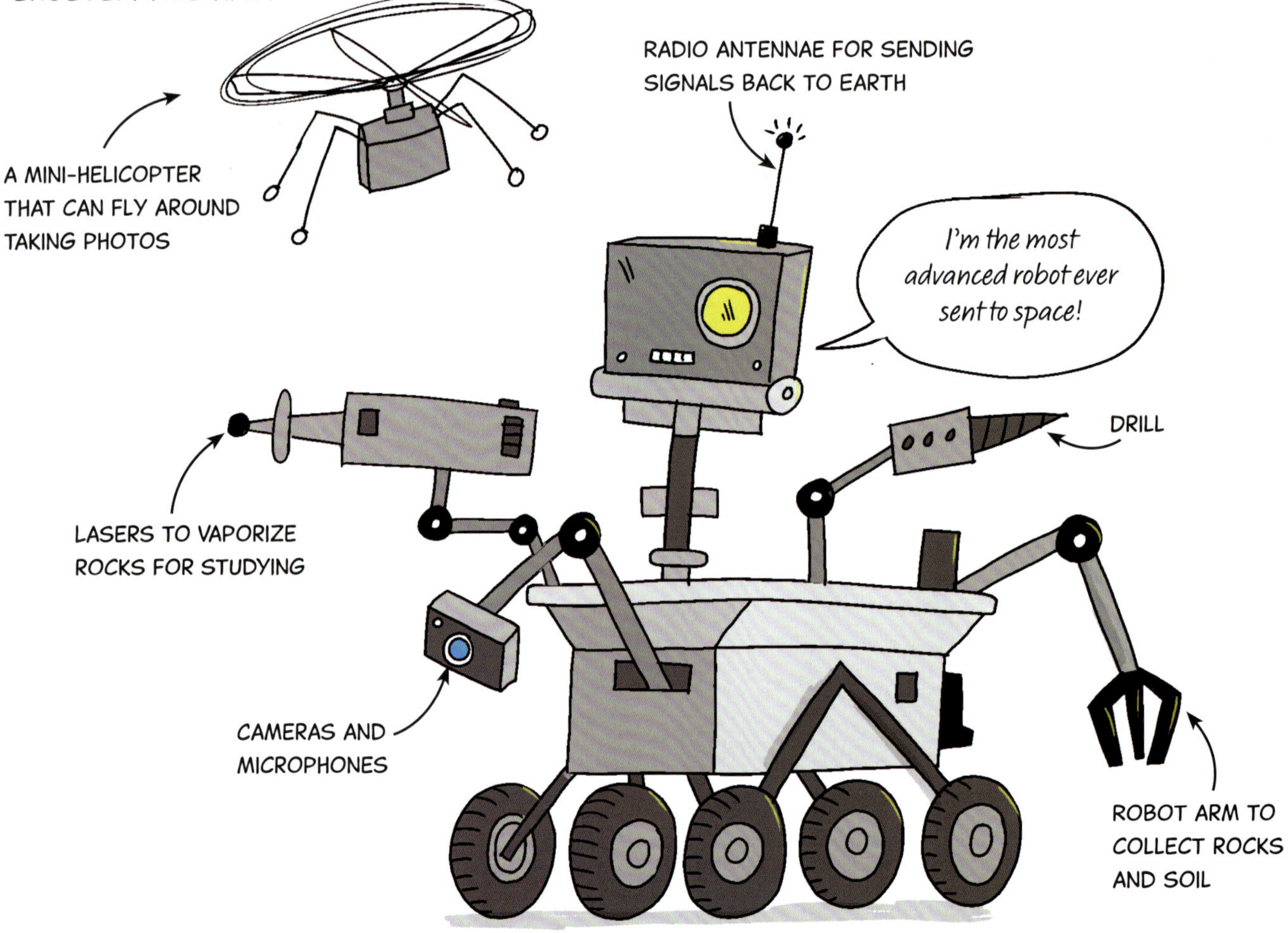
A MINI-HELICOPTER THAT CAN FLY AROUND TAKING PHOTOS
RADIO ANTENNAE FOR SENDING SIGNALS BACK TO EARTH
I'm the most advanced robot ever sent to space!
DRILL
LASERS TO VAPORIZE ROCKS FOR STUDYING
CAMERAS AND MICROPHONES
ROBOT ARM TO COLLECT ROCKS AND SOIL

DREAMING OF MARS

BUT COULD HUMANS GO TO MARS TOO, ONE DAY?

SPACE SCIENTISTS ARE PLANNING HUMAN MISSIONS TO MARS – BUT THERE ARE A LOT OF PROBLEMS TO SOLVE.

I'd love to be the first human on Mars! And you could be the first cat!
No, thanks! It sounds horrible!
BUILDING SAFE, ENCLOSED SHELTERS WITH AIR INSIDE ...
... POWER PLANTS FOR ELECTRICITY ...
... AND GREENHOUSES TO GROW FOOD.
Can I go home now?

SATELLITES SAVE THE DAY

ONE DAY, IN EARTH'S ORBIT ...
Hi, Hubble! How's the stargazing going?
Great, thanks!
EVERY DAY, THOUSANDS OF SATELLITES ARE ORBITING EARTH.
JUST THEN ...
There goes the space station!
Yoo hoo! Hi guys!
THE INTERNATIONAL SPACE STATION, OR ISS, IS A SATELLITE TOO.
BUT ...
Oh no! Looks like trouble! I hope the weather satellites have spotted it!
Don't panic! We're on it!
THESE TWO SATELLITES CIRCLE EARTH 14 TIMES A DAY, MEASURING THE CLOUDS AND TEMPERATURES.

I've got a lovely photo of it!
WEATHER SATELLITES CAN CAPTURE IMAGES OF CLOUDS AND STORMS, SUCH AS HURRICANES AND TYPHOONS ...
AND ...
I've got the temperatures. Hmm, that's a big, powerful storm! Could be dangerous!
...THEY CAN ALSO MEASURE TEMPERATURES ON LAND, IN THE SEA, AND IN THE ATMOSPHERE.
NEXT ...
Transmitting data ... hope they get it in time!
RADIO SIGNALS TRANSMIT THE INFORMATION BACK TO EARTH ...
Phew!
YIKES! Hurricane alert! Storm incoming! Evacuate the coast!
... HELPING US TO AVOID WEATHER DISASTERS!

EYES IN THE SKY

WHAT IS A SATELLITE?

A SATELLITE IS ANYTHING THAT ORBITS AROUND A SPACE OBJECT.

They're watching us right now!
What are?
The satellites!

EARTH IS A SATELLITE OF THE SUN ...

... AND THE MOON IS A SATELLITE OF EARTH!

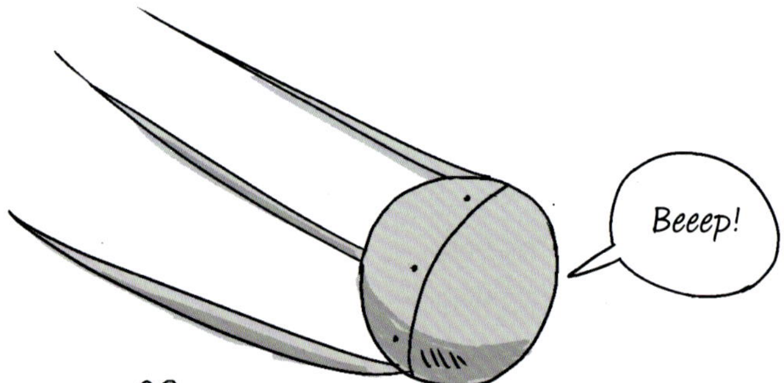
Beeep!

BUT SINCE THE 1950S, WE'VE BEEN BUILDING AND LUNCHING OUR OWN, HUMAN-MADE SATELLITES TOO ...

THE FIRST WAS SPUTNIK 1, LAUNCHED IN 1957

It was only the size of a washing machine!
And now there are over 7,000 of them!

WHAT ARE THEY FOR?

WE USE SATELLITES FOR A RANGE OF DIFFERENT, EXTREMELY USEFUL THINGS ...

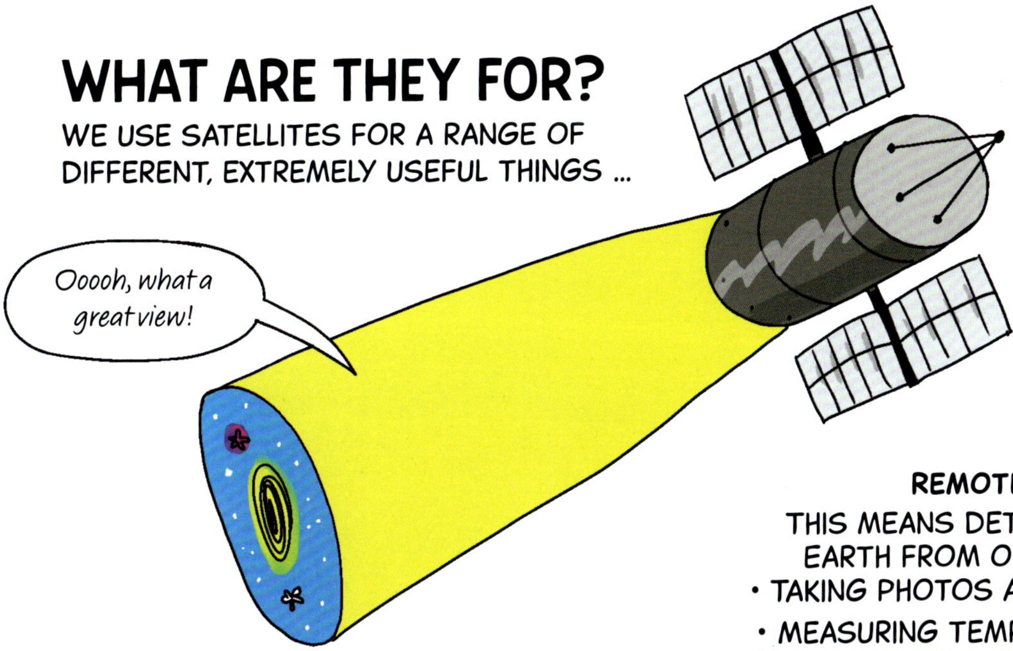
Ooooh, what a great view!

WATCHING THE STARS

IN ORBIT, THERE ARE NO CLOUDS IN THE WAY, SO SPACE TELESCOPES GET A GREAT VIEW OF THE SKY.

REMOTE SENSING

THIS MEANS DETECTING THINGS ON EARTH FROM ORBIT. IT INCLUDES:

- TAKING PHOTOS AND VIDEOS OF EARTH
- MEASURING TEMPERATURES, GASES IN THE ATMOSPHERE, HEIGHTS, AND DISTANCES
- SPOTTING STORMS, WILDFIRES, AND VOLCANIC ERUPTIONS

SENDING MESSAGES

COMMUNICATIONS OR "COMMS" SATELLITES BEAM INFORMATION AROUND THE WORLD, SUCH AS EMAILS FROM THE INTERNATIONAL SPACE STATION OR PHONE SIGNALS.

Handy for making maps, weather forecasting ...
... and spotting natural disasters!

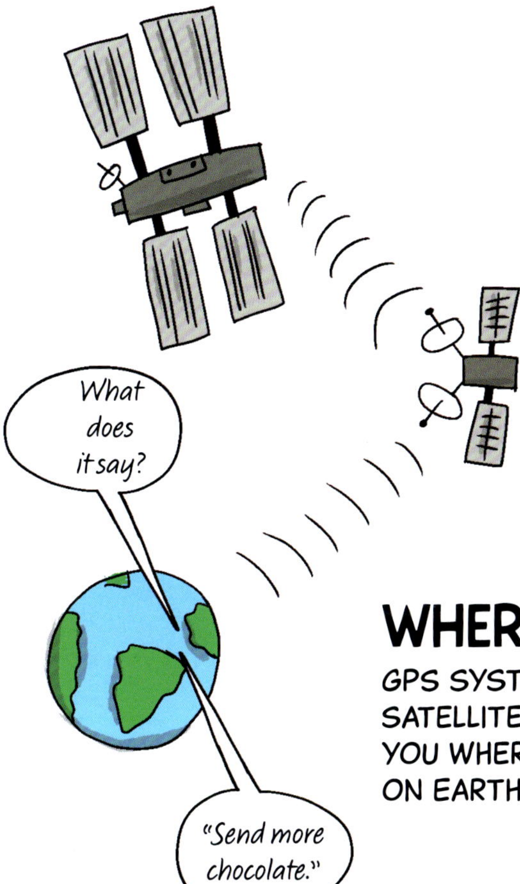
What does it say?
"Send more chocolate."

WHERE AM I?

GPS SYSTEMS USE SATELLITES TO SHOW YOU WHERE YOU ARE ON EARTH.

You are lost.
Not again!

IS THERE ANYBODY OUT THERE?

IN THE OUTER SOLAR SYSTEM ...
Beginning Saturn flyby!
A ROBOT SPACE PROBE FROM EARTH ARRIVES AT SATURN.
In Enceladus orbit...
THE PROBE ENTERS THE ORBIT OF ONE OF SATURN'S MOONS.
AND...
Landing successful!
ENCELADUS'S ICY SURFACE IS THOUGHT TO HAVE AN OCEAN OF LIQUID WATER UNDERNEATH.
UNDER THE ICE ...
What was that? Oh no – not those humans again!

Uh oh!!
THEN ...
It's drilled THROUGH the ice! Let's get out of here!
Starting ocean exploration!
Don't think it spotted us! Phew!
AND...
No signs of life on Enceladus! Beginning return sequence.
Good riddance! Fooled it again.

THE SEARCH FOR LIFE

Do other life forms exist out in space? Or are we alone in the universe?
Who knows? It's a mystery!

They really are clueless.

COULD ALIENS EXIST?

YES, THEY COULD! SCIENTISTS THINK THAT FOR LIFE TO EXIST, YOU NEED:

- LIQUID WATER

- INGREDIENTS FOR BUILDING CELLS, SUCH AS CARBON AND NITROGEN

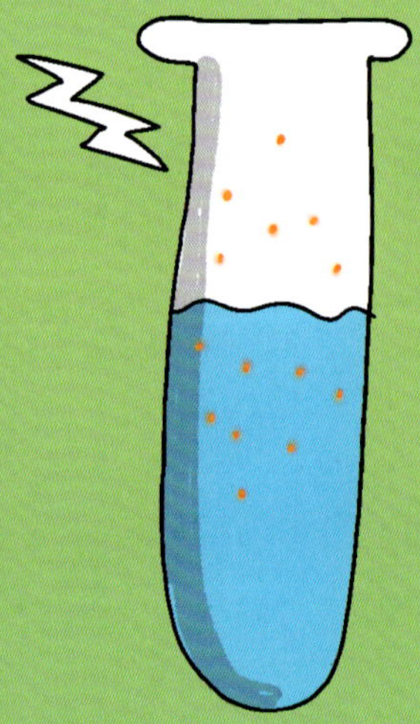

- HEAT, LIGHT, OR OTHER ENERGY

I'm alive!

SO WHERE ARE THEY?

WE'VE FOUND QUITE A FEW PLANETS AND MOONS THAT HAVE THESE THINGS – SO LIFE COULD HAVE STARTED THERE, LIKE IT DID ON EARTH.

THEY INCLUDE SOME OF JUPITER'S AND SATURN'S MOONS, LIKE ENCELADUS ...

Are there aliens here?

THE PLANETS MARS AND VENUS ...

Or maybe here?

AND SEVERAL PLANETS FAR AWAY IN SPACE, CALLED "EXOPLANETS." IF THEY'RE NOT TOO HOT AND NOT TOO COLD, THEY COULD BE JUST RIGHT FOR LIQUID WATER – AND LIFE!

That's why we're called "Goldilocks" planets!

The universe is so huge, life HAS to exist somewhere! At least, that's what I think!
Then why haven't any aliens visited us or sent a message?
Maybe they're small and simple, like bacteria – so they haven't invented any technology yet.
? ? ? ?

Or maybe they're too far away for us to find each other?
Or MAYBE they're super-smart, and they're just avoiding you!

GLOSSARY

ATOMS THE TINY UNITS THAT ALL MATTER IS MADE UP OF.

BACTERIA VERY SMALL, SINGLE-CELLED MICROORGANISMS, FOUND IN ALMOST EVERY HABITAT.

BIG BANG A SUDDEN EXPANSION AT THE START OF THE UNIVERSE, WHEN EVERYTHING BEGAN TO EXIST.

BLACK HOLE A POINT IN SPACE THAT CONTAINS A HUGE AMOUNT OF MATTER AND HAS VERY POWERFUL GRAVITY.

ECLIPSE A SHADOW CAST BY ONE SPACE OBJECT, SUCH AS A PLANET OR MOON, ONTO ANOTHER.

EXOPLANETS PLANETS THAT EXIST OUTSIDE OUR OWN SOLAR SYSTEM.

GALAXY A HUGE CLUSTER OF MILLIONS OR BILLIONS OF STARS.

GRAVITY A FORCE THAT ALL OBJECTS HAVE, THAT PULLS OTHER OBJECTS TOWARD THEM.

HURRICANE A LARGE, SWIRLING WINDSTORM IN THE ATLANTIC OR NORTHEASTERN PACIFIC OCEAN.

LASER A DEVICE THAT GIVES OUT A NARROW, POWERFUL BEAM OF LIGHT.

MICROGRAVITY A SENSATION OF WEIGHTLESSNESS OR ZERO GRAVITY, CAUSED BY BEING IN ORBIT.

ORBIT THE PATH OF ONE OBJECT IN SPACE, SUCH AS A MOON, AROUND ANOTHER, SUCH AS A PLANET.

POLES (NORTH POLE AND SOUTH POLE) THE MOST NORTHERN AND SOUTHERN POINTS ON EARTH. EARTH SPINS AROUND THE LINE BETWEEN THE TWO POLES.

REMOTE SENSING SCANNING EARTH USING SATELLITES TO CREATE IMAGES OR MAPS OR COLLECT INFORMATION.

SATELLITE AN OBJECT THAT ORBITS AROUND EARTH, OR AROUND ANOTHER OBJECT IN SPACE.

SOLAR SYSTEM THE SUN AND ALL THE PLANETS, MOONS, AND OTHER SPACE OBJECTS THAT ORBIT AROUND IT.

SPACE PROBE A SMALL SPACECRAFT WITH NO CREW, SENT FROM EARTH TO EXPLORE SPACE OBJECTS.

SUPERNOVA A HUGE EXPLOSION THAT HAPPENS WHEN VERY BIG STARS GET OLD.

TYPHOON A LARGE, SWIRLING WINDSTORM IN THE NORTHWESTERN PACIFIC OCEAN.

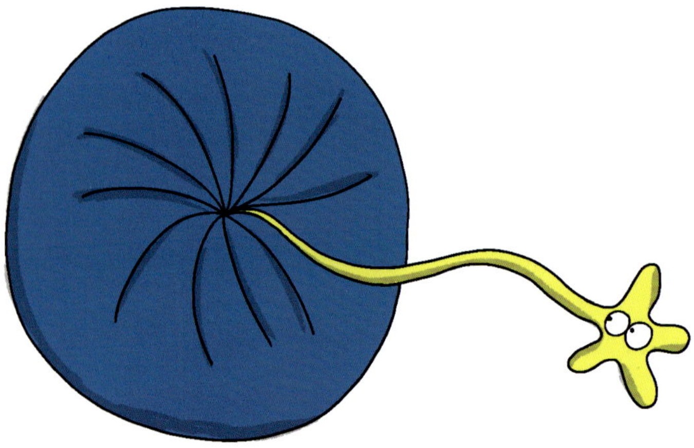

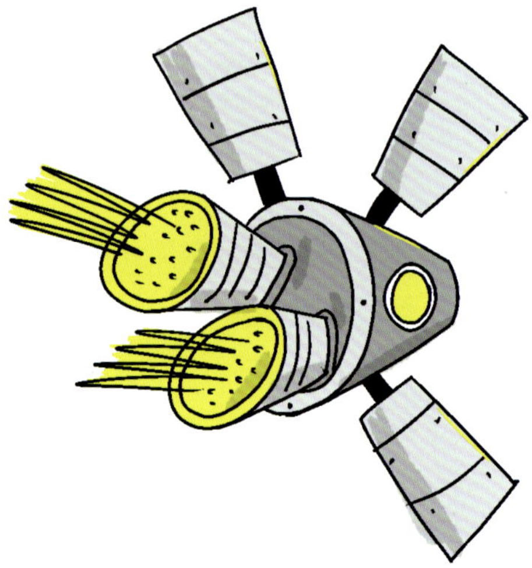

QUIZ

1. WHAT DO SCIENTISTS THINK HAPPENED WHEN THE UNIVERSE BEGAN?

A. THE BIG BONG

B. THE BIG BOOM

C. THE BIG BANG

2. WHO DISCOVERED THAT THE PLANET JUPITER HAS MOONS?

A. GALEN

B. GALILEO

C. GARFIELD

3. WHAT KIND OF FORCE IS GRAVITY?

A. A PULLING FORCE

B. A PUSHING FORCE

C. A SQUEEZING FORCE

4. WHAT IS BETELGEUSE?

A. A GINORMOUS GALAXY

B. A GINORMOUS STAR

C. A GINORMOUS SPACESHIP

5. WHAT HAPPENS TO A STAR THAT GETS SUCKED INTO A BLACK HOLE?

A. IT GETS BROKEN INTO TINY PIECES

B. IT GETS FLATTENED LIKE A PANCAKE

C. IT GETS STRETCHED OUT LIKE SPAGHETTI

6. WHICH OF THESE MUSICAL INSTRUMENTS HAS NOT BEEN PLAYED ON THE INTERNATIONAL SPACE STATION?

A. A GUITAR

B. A GRAND PIANO

C. A SAXOPHONE

7. WHICH PLANET ARE HUMANS PLANNING TO VISIT FIRST?

A. MARS

B. MERCURY

C. JUPITER

8. WHAT WAS THE FIRST ARTIFICIAL SATELLITE CALLED?

A. BEATNIK

B. SPUTNIK

C. PICNIC

9. DO ALIENS EXIST?

A. YES

B. NO

C. NOBODY KNOWS

10. WHAT DO SCIENTISTS THINK EXISTED BEFORE THE BIG BANG?

A. THE SUN

B. NOTHING

C. A FEW ATOMS

ANSWERS: 1. C, 2. B, 3. A, 4. B, 5. C, 6. B, 7. A, 8. B, 9. C, 10. B

INDEX